NOAH'S ARK

This Book
Belongs
to

. . . .

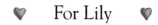

♥   For Lily   ♥

Illustrations © 1988 by Sophie Windham

First published 1988 by
MACMILLAN CHILDREN'S BOOKS
A division of Macmillan Publishers Limited
London and Basingstoke
Associated companies throughout the world

Picturemac edition published 1990

Produced for the Publishers by
Sadie Fields Productions Limited, London

ISBN 0-333-53938-9

A CIP catalogue record for this book is available from the British Library

Printed in Hong Kong

NOAH'S ARK

Sophie Windham

MACMILLAN CHILDREN'S BOOKS

Noah was behaving strangely.

Sometimes he would look up and nod.

Sometimes he would look down and frown.

And all the time he seemed to be talking to himself.

But Mrs. Noah said nothing until one day . . .

"It's going to rain," said Noah."We've got to build a boat!"

"Wouldn't an umbrella do?" asked Mrs. Noah.

"Not a thousand umbrellas! And not a moment to lose!
It's going to rain, and rain, and rain!"

Outside the wind blew and blew and blew.

Inside, Noah made his plans.

When he had finished,

Mrs. Noah brought them tea and

Noah showed her what he had done.

"There's going to be a mighty flood," said Noah.

"When the rains come, even the tops of the highest
mountains will be covered by the sea!"

"People have not taken care of the world.

We have been chosen to save the animals and

I must build an ark for them which will float on the water."

And Noah chose the strongest trees and sawed the

wood into planks and began to build his ark.

At last it was finished and Noah said to Mrs. Noah,

"Now we must bring together every kind of animal in the world."

There were so many animals to find –

stripey ones and spotty ones and muddy ones.

They chose two of every kind,

a male and a female of each.

Shiny ones and hairy ones and bald ones.

ry ones and bald ones.

They chose tw

a male and a fe

And two by two they came to Noah's ark,

which was finished just in time.

Mrs. Noah had stocked the ark with

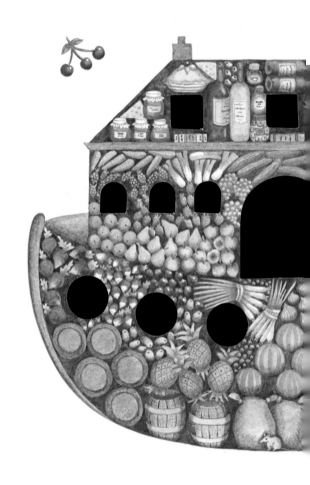

so there was enough for

At last Noah and Mrs. Noah and the animals were safely inside.

No sooner were they settled than

a great black cloud hid the sun.

And the windows of heaven opened

and rain poured down.

And soon,

puddles formed pools.

Pools became lakes.

And lakes became seas.

And when the seas joined together, the ark

floated up on dark and angry waters covering the land.

For forty days and forty nights it rained.

Storms followed gales, and gales followed storms.

Until, at last, the storm became a shower and the shower became a mist,

and then there was only a single raindrop . . .

The next morning, a beautiful light woke Noah and his wife.

It was the sun! The wonderful yellow sun! They dressed and hurried outside.
A rainbow soared across the sky. But for as far as the tallest giraffe could see,

there was nothing but water. So Noah sent a dove to explore
and, in the evening, she returned with a tiny new olive leaf in her beak.

"We are saved!" cried Noah. "The animals are saved!

And the trees and flowers! The world is saved!"

All the creatures in the ark called out in thanks.

"I did not realise how beautiful the flowers are –
even the smallest of them – until they disappeared," said Noah.

"The world is a beautiful place," said Mrs. Noah,

"and the animals and plants make it so.

We must never risk losing it again."

Other Picturemacs you will enjoy

THE GRASS IS GREENER   Jez Alborough
THE KING'S FLOWER   Mitsumasa Anno
JACK AND NANCY   Quentin Blake
FRANKLIN IN THE DARK   Paulette Bourgeois/Brenda Clark
NUNGU AND THE CROCODILE   Babette Cole
I'LL TAKE YOU TO MRS COLE   Nigel Gray/Michael Foreman
AARDVARK'S PICNIC   Jon Atlas Higham
AESOP'S FABLES   Heidi Holder
THE MICE NEXT DOOR   Anthony Knowles/Susan Edwards
A PORCUPINE NAMED FLUFFY   Helen Lester/Lynn Munsinger
DRAGON FOR BREAKFAST   Eunice and Nigel McMullen
HARRY'S NIGHT OUT   Abigail Pizer
NOSEY GILBERT   Abigail Pizer
HENRIETTA GOOSE   Abigail Pizer
MR AND MRS PIG'S EVENING OUT   Mary Rayner
GARTH PIG AND THE ICECREAM LADY   Mary Rayner
MRS PIG'S BULK BUY   Mary Rayner
ALISTAIR'S TIME MACHINE   Marilyn Sadler/Roger Bollen
IMOGENE'S ANTLERS   David Small
DOLLY — THE STORY OF A LONDON MOUSE   Jenny Thorne
THE PIRATE PIG   Anne Tyrrell/Cathie Shuttleworth
THE BEAR'S WINTER HOUSE   John Yeoman/Quentin Blake
THE BEAR'S WATER PICNIC   John Yeoman/Quentin Blake
BEATRICE AND VANESSA   John Yeoman/Quentin Blake

For a complete list of Picturemac titles write to:

Macmillan Children's Books,
18—21 Cavaye Place, London SW10 9PG